WHO HQ
AF386822

To Betsy Laskowski—a true football scholar—EL

For Özgün, my partner in endless sports
documentary binges—AB

PENGUIN WORKSHOP
An imprint of Penguin Random House LLC
1745 Broadway, New York, NY 10019
penguinrandomhouse.com

Design by Taylor Abatiell
Text set in Adobe Garamond Pro

The art was created using Procreate for sketching and Adobe Photoshop for colors, utilizing various textured digital brushes.

Library of Congress Cataloging-in-Publication Data is available.

First published in the United States of America by Penguin Workshop, 2026

Manufactured in China
HH

ISBN 9798217144259
10 9 8 7 6 5 4 3 2 1

The authorized representative in the EU for product safety and compliance is Penguin Random House Ireland, Morrison Chambers, 32 Nassau Street, Dublin D02 YH68, Ireland, https://eu-contact.penguin.ie.

THE KELCE BROTHERS

A WHO HQ ILLUSTRATED BIOGRAPHY

by
Ellen Labrecque

illustrated by
Alexandra Badiu

PENGUIN WORKSHOP

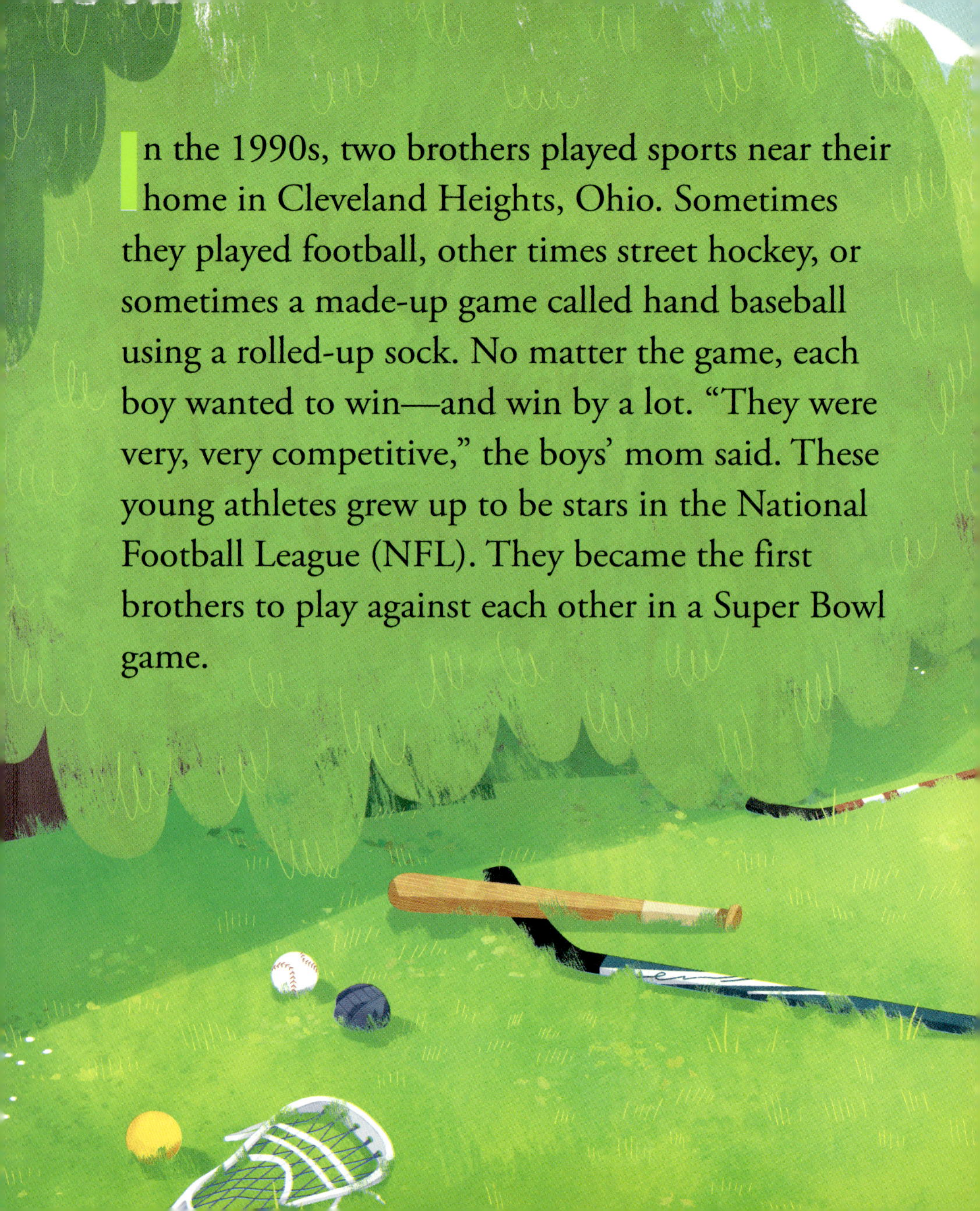

In the 1990s, two brothers played sports near their home in Cleveland Heights, Ohio. Sometimes they played football, other times street hockey, or sometimes a made-up game called hand baseball using a rolled-up sock. No matter the game, each boy wanted to win—and win by a lot. "They were very, very competitive," the boys' mom said. These young athletes grew up to be stars in the National Football League (NFL). They became the first brothers to play against each other in a Super Bowl game.

WHO WERE THESE FUTURE SUPERSTARS?

Jason Daniel Kelce was born on November 5, 1987. His younger brother, Travis Michael Kelce, was born two years later on October 5, 1989. Their mother, Donna, worked at a bank and their father, Ed, worked at a steel mill.

The boys were energetic and rowdy growing up. "We were always in the backyard, whether it was playing basketball or even home-run derby with wiffle ball bats," explained Jason.

When it was too cold to play outside, the brothers played hockey in their basement. Jason and Travis were the best of friends, but also the fiercest of rivals.

"There were a lot of fights," Donna said. "It all just stemmed from somebody being better than the other one, and the other one not being able to deal with it."

As Cleveland Heights High School students, Jason played football, ice hockey, and baseball, and Travis played football, basketball, and baseball. Jason was a running back and linebacker on the football team, and Travis played quarterback. They were exceptional athletes—especially Travis. "Travis was the only individual I've known in twenty-eight years as a coach that could have been a Division I college football, baseball or basketball player," said Jeff Rotsky, his high school football coach.

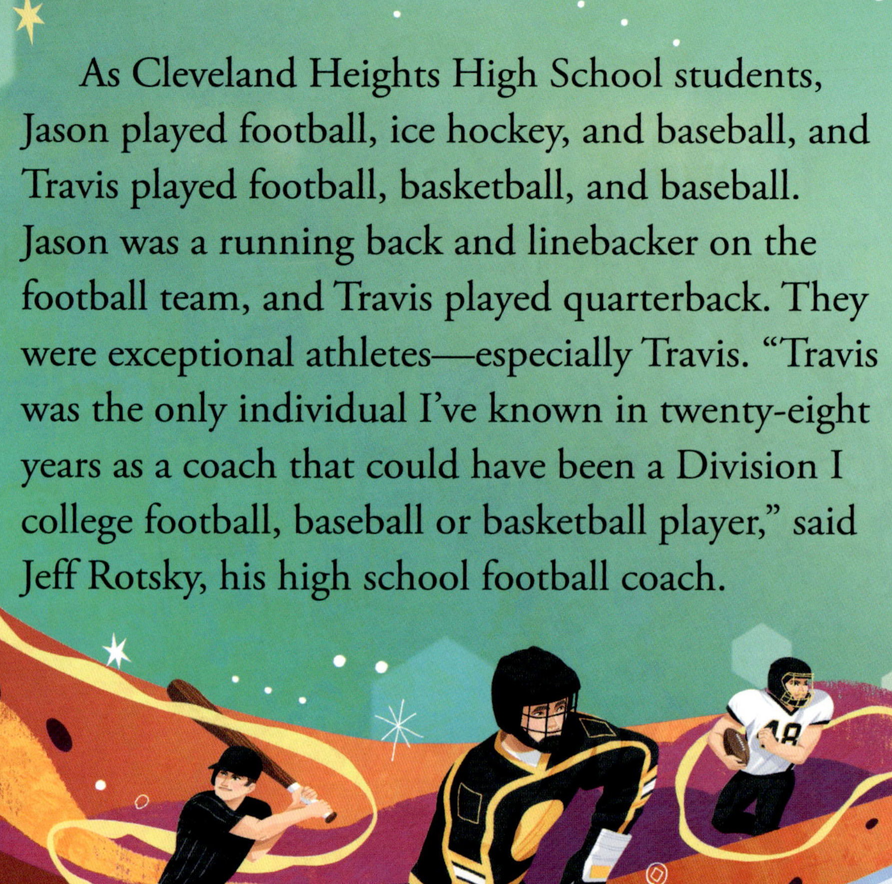

The boys were both big and tall. Jason stands at six feet, three inches and Travis is six feet, five inches. They also had big frames. They ate a lot of food to stay fueled for competition.

"They could sit down and eat an entire chicken . . . not together; each one of them could finish a chicken," said Donna.

Jason went to the University of Cincinnati to play football after high school. His coach switched his position to the offensive line. Jason eventually became the team's starting center. A center's job is to think about strategy. They read the defense and protect the quarterback. Jason said the position switch was "the single greatest move that ever happened to me as a football player."

Two years later, in 2008, Travis followed his big brother to the same university. And just like Jason, Travis eventually switched his position, too. He went from quarterback to tight end. A tight end has a lot of roles. On some plays, the tight end runs downfield to catch the ball like a receiver. On others, he helps the other linemen protect the quarterback.

After college, in 2011, Jason was chosen by the Philadelphia Eagles in the NFL Draft. He was selected in the sixth round—the 191st pick. Other teams passed on him because of his size. Even though Jason weighed 280 pounds, teams thought he wasn't big enough. The average weight of an NFL center is 30 or even 40 pounds heavier than Jason was. "There was a lot of doubt whether I could play at the next level," said Jason. He wanted to prove all those other teams wrong.

The Kansas City Chiefs drafted Travis two years later in the third round—the 63rd overall pick. Travis had also hoped to be selected a lot higher than he was. But when Coach Andy Reid of the Kansas City Chiefs called, Travis projected confidence. Travis told his future coach he would be the team's best tight end. Coach Reid believed him.

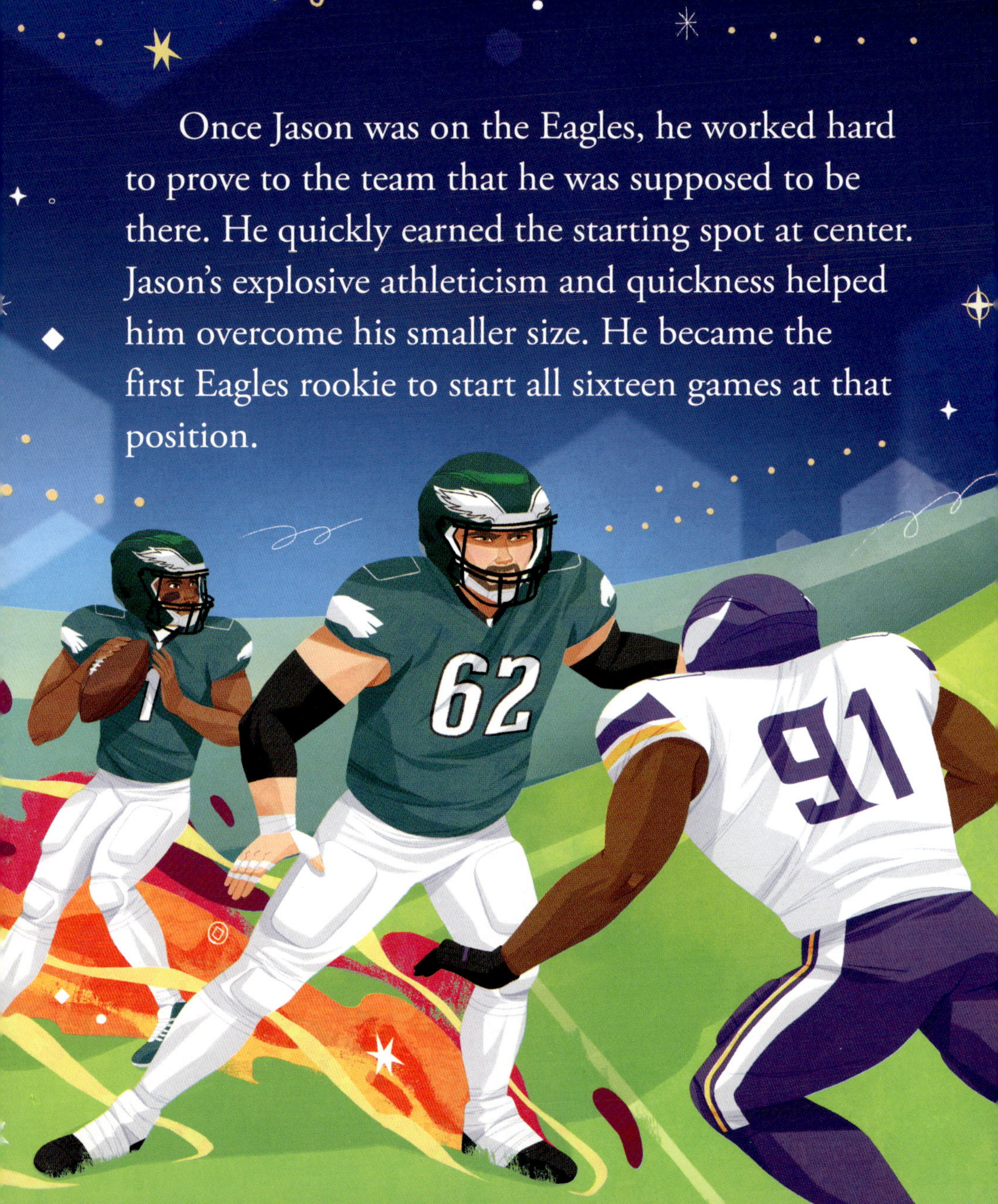

Once Jason was on the Eagles, he worked hard to prove to the team that he was supposed to be there. He quickly earned the starting spot at center. Jason's explosive athleticism and quickness helped him overcome his smaller size. He became the first Eagles rookie to start all sixteen games at that position.

When Travis joined the Chiefs, he wore the number 87. He chose it because it was the year Jason was born. Travis had followed his older brother everywhere—and now to the NFL! "I don't think I'm the same athlete without my brother," Travis said. "Every time I put on the jersey, that gives me something to represent."

Jason became a Philadelphia fan favorite almost immediately. Fans loved his hardworking ethic and his will to win. They also liked that Jason seemed like a regular guy. He wore sweatpants and flip-flops when he showed up for games. Jason was a great teammate, too. His job was to protect and to make the players around him look good—**AND HE DID JUST THAT.**

Travis became a beloved player in Kansas City, too. But he was different from his older brother. Travis loved getting dressed up and wearing fancy clothes to games. Travis was flashy on the field, too. He performed fun dances in the end zone when he caught a pass for a touchdown. "I get into the end zone and I turn into this happy-go-lucky kid," he said.

In 2017, Jason had his best season as a professional player. He started in all sixteen games and led the Eagles to a 13–3 regular season record. This was tied for most regular season wins in franchise history. Jason was also selected as First Team All-Pro. This means he was considered the best center in the entire NFL.

In the postseason, the Eagles made it to Super Bowl LII (52). Travis's season ended in the playoffs, so he came to the game in Minneapolis to support his brother. Philadelphia defeated the New England Patriots, 41–33, for the team's first-ever Super Bowl victory. Jason made a rousing speech at the victory parade in Philadelphia after the Super Bowl. He asked the boisterous crowd to scream if they loved the Philadelphia Eagles. **AND THEY SURE DID SCREAM!**

By 2018, Travis had developed into one of the best tight ends in the NFL. But unlike his brother Jason's team, the Chiefs had not reached the Super Bowl. Things changed when the Chiefs began starting quarterback Patrick Mahomes, who had been drafted a year earlier. Patrick and Travis soon became a winning dynamic duo together!

In 2020, two years after Jason and the Eagles won the Super Bowl, the Chiefs made it. This time, Jason cheered on Travis. Kansas City beat the San Francisco 49ers in Super Bowl LIV (54), 31–20. Travis caught six passes for forty-three yards and one touchdown! During the Chiefs' celebration parade in Kansas City, Travis made a speech just like his brother. "Can you dig it?" Travis screamed to the crowd.

THE SUPER BOWL

The Super Bowl is the NFL's annual championship game between the winners of its two conferences—the National Football Conference (NFC) and the American Football Conference (AFC). The reason the NFL has two conferences is because there used to be two professional football leagues (the National Football League and the American Football League). In 1970, after Super Bowl IV (4), the leagues merged. Today, each conference is made up of sixteen teams. At the end of the regular season, each conference has their own playoffs until one team is crowned the conference champion. These champions then face each other in the Super Bowl.

The Super Bowl is the most-watched and hyped event in all of American entertainment! Over 127 million fans watched in 2025! The game takes place in a different US city every year—usually in a warm location such as Miami, Florida, or New Orleans, Louisiana. The Super Bowl uses Roman numerals. For instance, the Super Bowl in February 2025 was Super Bowl LIX (59). The Super Bowl name was coined in 1966 by Lamar Hunt, who owned the Kansas City Chiefs for almost five decades. He came up with the name when his kids were playing with a toy called a Super Ball. He decided to call the game the Super Bowl.

By the fall of 2022, Jason, and especially Travis, had become very famous. So much so that the brothers decided to do a podcast together. They called it *New Heights*—a clever tribute to their hometown, Cleveland Heights. On the podcast, the brothers joked around with each other, talked about childhood memories, and gave insight on NFL players and games. The podcast quickly became one of the top-rated sports podcasts.

That same season, Kansas City won the AFC championship and Philadelphia won the NFC championship. This meant the brothers' teams would face each other in the Super Bowl.

IT'D BE THE FIRST TIME IN NFL HISTORY THAT A PAIR OF BROTHERS WOULD BATTLE EACH OTHER ON THE FIELD IN THE BIG GAME!

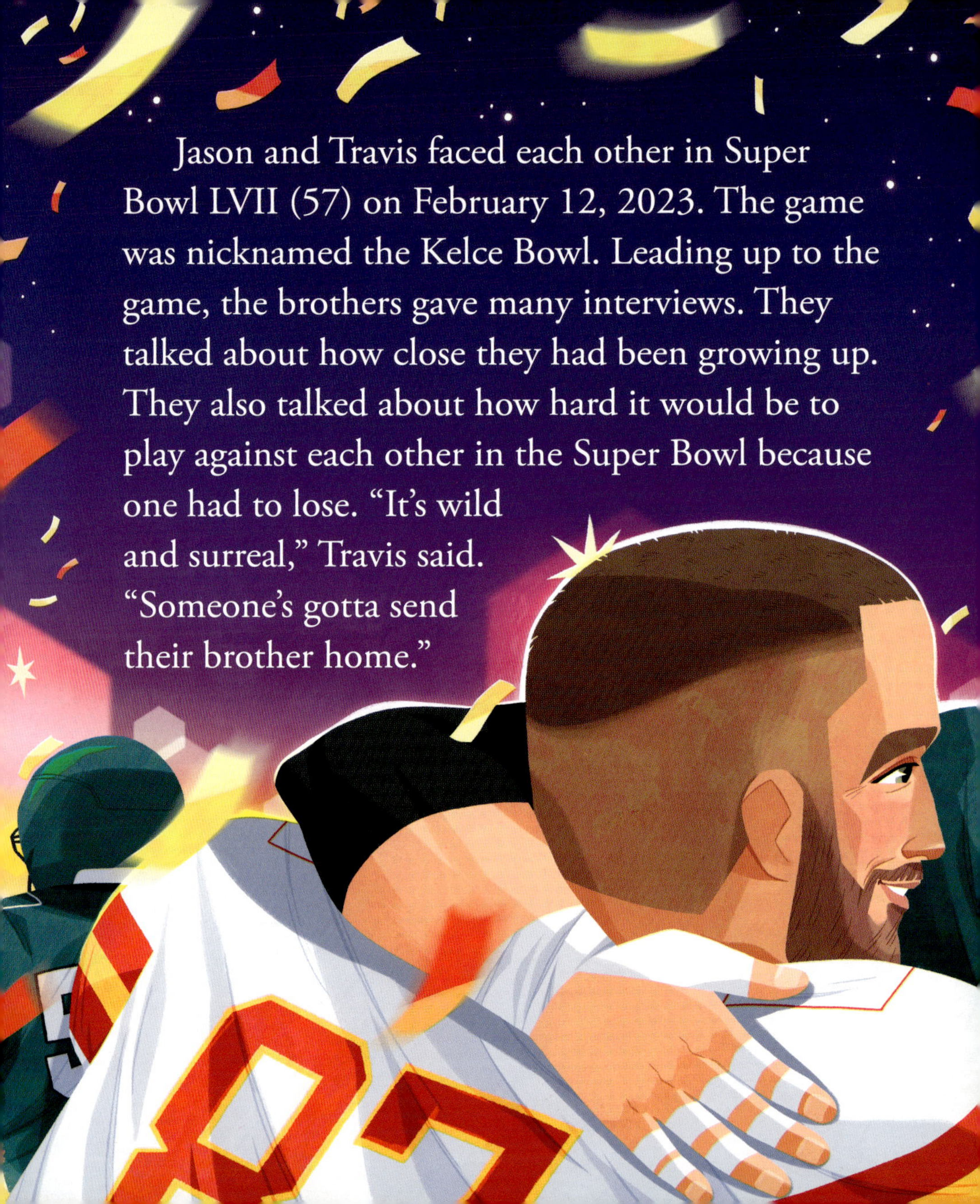

Jason and Travis faced each other in Super Bowl LVII (57) on February 12, 2023. The game was nicknamed the Kelce Bowl. Leading up to the game, the brothers gave many interviews. They talked about how close they had been growing up. They also talked about how hard it would be to play against each other in the Super Bowl because one had to lose. "It's wild and surreal," Travis said. "Someone's gotta send their brother home."

Travis scored the first touchdown of the game. He caught an eighteen-yard reception and then did a joyful dance. The Eagles fought back and with ten seconds to play, the score was tied, 35–35. The Chiefs kicked a field goal and won the game, 38–35. Travis won his second Super Bowl. Jason was disappointed for himself, but supportive of his sibling—just like an older brother should be. "I'm really happy for Trav and the Chiefs," he said.

In March 2024, Jason retired. He had played thirteen seasons in the league and had played the most career games of any offensive lineman in Eagles history. He also had the most consecutive starts (156). During his retirement speech, Jason thanked his teammates and fans and also said, "There is no chance I'd be here without the bond Travis and I share. It made me stronger, tougher, smarter."

Jason soon signed a three-year deal with
ESPN, landing a prime spot as a television analyst
on *Monday Night Countdown*. He also began
spending a lot more time with his family. Jason
and his wife, Kylie, have four daughters. "Kylie and
Jason are just unbelievable parents," said Travis.

In the summer of 2023, Travis began dating Taylor Swift, one of the most famous musicians in the world. Fans followed the couple's every move. They even had a nickname for them—*Tayvis.* Travis, though, still had more football to play! In 2024, at Super Bowl LVIII (58), he helped lead the Chiefs back to a Super Bowl victory. They beat the San Francisco 49ers again, this time in overtime, 25–22.

The very next season, the Chiefs made it back to the Super Bowl again and were hoping to become the first team ever to win three consecutive Super Bowls. This time, though, in Super Bowl LIX (59), they lost to the Eagles, 40–22. Travis was disappointed but also knew how lucky he was. Just six months later, he became engaged to Taylor! "I have a beautiful life," Travis said.

Becoming an NFL star is an incredible accomplishment for one player. But when two siblings become Super Bowl winners and future Football Hall of Famers? *Unbelievable!* Jason and Travis were always there for each other—in every tackle, block, and catch—along the way. They will probably never play professional football together again, but one thing is for sure: **THEY'LL ALWAYS BE THE BEST OF BROTHERS.**

BIBLIOGRAPHY

***Books for young readers**

*Anderson, Josh. ***Inside the Kansas City Chiefs***. Minneapolis, MN: Lerner Sports Publishing, 2023.

Argott, Don, director. ***Kelce***. Amazon Prime Video, 2023.

*Jordan, Apple. ***The Kelce Brothers: A Little Golden Book Biography***. New York: Golden Books, 2024.

Salters, Lisa. "Bond of Brothers: Travis and Jason Kelce." ***E:60***. ESPN. July 27, 2018.

Sports Illustrated Kids*, editors. ***Big Book of WHO: Football*. Chicago: Triumph Books, 2022.

WEBSITES

www.chiefs.com

www.nfl.com

www.philadelphiaeagles.com

TIMELINE

1987	Jason Daniel Kelce is born on November 5
1989	Travis Michael Kelce is born on October 5
2006	Jason goes to the University of Cincinnati to play football and eventually becomes the team's center
2008	Travis goes to the University of Cincinnati to play quarterback and eventually becomes the team's tight end
2011	Jason is drafted by the Philadelphia Eagles
2013	Travis is drafted by the Kansas City Chiefs

Jason helps lead the Eagles to their first-ever Super Bowl title, beating the New England Patriots in Super Bowl LII (52)
2018
Travis and the Kansas City Chiefs beat the San Francisco 49ers in Super Bowl LIV (54)
2020
The brothers' podcast, New Heights, makes its debut
2022
Pitted against each other in a game dubbed the Kelce Bowl, the Chiefs defeat the Eagles in Super Bowl LVII (57)
2023
Travis and the Chiefs win their second Super Bowl in a row, beating the San Francisco 49ers in overtime
2024
Jason retires from the Eagles after thirteen seasons in the league
Jason becomes a television football analyst
Travis and the Chiefs lose Super Bowl LIX (59) to the Philadelphia Eagles
2025